Ruin & Want

Sundress Publications • Knoxville, TN

Copyright © 2023 by José Angel Araguz
ISBN: 978-1-951979-53-9
LCCN: 2023945459
Published by Sundress Publications
www.sundresspublications.com

Editor: Samantha Edmonds
Managing Editor: Tennison Black
Editorial Assistant: Erin Elizabeth Smith
Editorial Interns: Izzy Astuto, Heather Domenicis, Annie Fay Meitchik, K Slade

Colophon: This book is set in Playfair Display Medium
Cover Art: Ani Araguz
Cover Design: Kristen Ton
Book Design: Samantha Edmonds

"may i feel said he" Copyright 1935, (c) 1963, 1991 by the Trustees for the E. E. Cummings Trust.
Copyright (c) 1978 by George James Firmage, from *COMPLETE POEMS: 1904-1962* by E. E. Cummings, edited by George J. Firmage. Used by permission of Liveright Publishing Corporation.

Ruin & Want

José Angel Araguz

Acknowledgments

The author wishes to thank the editors of the following journals in which excerpts from this manuscript, sometimes in alternate versions, first appeared:

Blue Earth Review (as "excerpts from 'The Seven Sins of Want: attention/admission'")

Treehouse (as "The devil on his wedding night")

The Acentos Review (as "excerpts from *A Personal History of Want* 'ch. 1'")

Storm Cellar (as "excerpts from *A Personal History of Want* 'ch. 3 & 5'")

Table of Contents

[one]	1
[two]	21
[three]	39
[four]	67
[five] Devil or Nothing: An Abandoned Manuscript	87
[six]	117
[seven]	131
Epilogue	157
Notes	171
About the Author	173

for Jojo & Jesse

[one]

Perhaps to make nice while visiting New York, L decides to treat me and my then-girlfriend to a Broadway show. This during grad school, which I remember only as stages of exhaustion: working mornings at a coffee shop in the city; sitting through classes at night; spending the time in between worrying about what I was doing with my life.

Years since L and I last saw each other in person, I am still the brooding student, and she the benevolent teacher. Looking back, I can empathize with the impulse to be benevolent. As a teacher, you want to encourage and support, make another human aware of their potential, hoping they won't waste as much time as you did full of doubt.

Perhaps that's why she reached out to me back in high school: my world was all doubt then. Perhaps that's where the good lies in all that happened between us, that someone took the time to see beyond my adolescent posturing to the real fear I had of not having a future. For the first time I saw myself as someone worth seeing.

Perhaps this is me lost in the moment again.

The moment when, as I make my way back to my seat after intermission, I look up to see L's face alive with a smile that knocks me down into my own smile for I-don't-know how long.

And the moment when I recover and find my then-girlfriend next to me in tears.

Wanting my then-girlfriend to no longer be mad, I say the moment meant nothing, that it was L just being weird, that I was just playing along.

Later I will know the word dissociation.

Right now, I only know the word *sorry*: that I played along. That I accepted the invitation to the musical. That I didn't find a way out of it.

It didn't help that the musical had a recurring song that repeated the name of the main love interest, the same name as L's real name. That we sat there, the three of us in the dark about each other, while an obsessive love played out in front of us.

Disgusted. My then-girlfriend is disgusted with me. She was once one of the people who knew about L and me (that we had had an affair that started when I was L's student, when I was 17 and she was 47) and had an intrusive if reserved curiosity about it. But now, only disgust.

Later, after being married for less than a year, I will recognize this look again from her when I ask for a divorce.

Right now, I just want my then-girlfriend to look at me with trust again. I want to take all the pain this night caused and hide it behind the curtains that closed at the end of the show, leaving us in a harsh light blinking back to our lives.

Wanting to be transparent, let me say I wish I didn't have to write this book. I wish there wasn't a need for survivors to tell their stories, to depict and re-engage with wounding experiences, that it was enough to survive.

Wanting to be transparent, let me share I wish I could tell this story in a straight line. I wish it was just a story, not a series of events that my mind can't help but try to shape into a story, however imperfect and incomplete.

Because none of the above wishes can be granted, I find it important to state this is my own recollection of events. Any omissions or errors made are on me. Working with memory risks flaws, flaws I'm happy to own on the path to evoking some of what happened. Small changes have been made to provide anonymity for others who might find themselves reflected in any of the narratives within.

Transparency: I get caught staring at how the word *spare* is held there in the middle, simultaneously said and visible while also unsaid and invisible.

I write these words so one day I can hold them to the light and begin to see what is behind them.

During our last in-person conversation, my ex-wife who had met L in NYC leans back, looks me in the eye, and says: *You know, Dante sent cheaters to Hell, right?*

Later, I can't remember if I had a response. I only remember her eyes, wide, searching for what some part of me might fear.

Want to write a book about L.

Want to write a book about how L manipulates me.

Want to write a book about a white woman preying upon a brown boy.

Want to write a book about Corpus Christi's social, racial, and economic dysfunctions as embodied in a predatory relationship.

Every time I try, I find myself looking over my shoulder.

Never want to write the book she wants me to, something glorifying her, but made so vague that she would be both celebrated and, at the same time, kept secret.

L gifts me a copy of James Joyce's *Dubliners,* says to read "Araby," tasks me to find her favorite line.

In the back of her minivan parked on the beach, L takes my teenage hand and slips it under her dress, whispers: *Do you feel how wet I am?*

I do and I don't.

I do in that my body is present, and I don't in that I am unsure what I am allowed to feel.

I do in that I have heard this played out in movies and stories from friends, and I don't in that I am surprised to see her eyes waiting for a response.

I do in that I have been wanting this kind of scene to play out with a woman, fantasized and gotten lost in thought thinking about it, and I don't in that I find myself not having the focus of fantasy—I can hear the ocean crashing, I can hear car doors open and close in the distance, I am worried I sprayed on too much *Cool Water* because it is all I can smell, and I cannot stop thinking that I should have had a response to what she said on the drive here: *I have great breasts, just wait!*

I do in that her eyes have a vulnerability to them that I have not seen before, a drop of the control and charm, and I don't in that I feel responsible for what has changed and yet in control of nothing.

I don't in that, when years have passed, I still will be unsure what this one moment means, and I do because I must find the words for what I feel.

Wanting closure and understanding, I talk about L to others.

Guys pat me on the back, say things like, *It must've been sweet!*

One guy says he didn't know "Hot for Teacher" was a real thing.

Some people look deeper into my eyes, perhaps trying to see what L sees in me.

No one calls it trauma.

No one calls it sexual assault.

No one calls it grooming.

No one calls it inappropriate.

The most familiar reaction from anyone is an awkward, heated silence, so much like the one the whole affair leaves me in, listening as words uselessly and recklessly spin out of me, until done, until all is silence.

"I thought little of the future. I did not know whether I would ever speak to her or not or, if I spoke to her, how I could tell her of my confused adoration. But my body was like a harp and her words and gestures were like fingers running upon the wires."
 —James Joyce, "Araby"

Want to tell L right away that I read the words, have found what I feel she wanted me to find, am flushed with the good-student thrill of it, but I spend the night instead worried I am wrong as I do the dishes, take out the trash, clean up after my siblings, play my guitar during commercial breaks while watching reruns on *Nick at Nite*, lock and relock the front door at least eight times before going to bed.

After class, L shares "The Ruined Maid" by Thomas Hardy, looking up as she recites the refrains from memory:

> *"O didn't you know I'd been ruined?" said she*

Later I will remember loving how much she smiles running through the ruins

> *"Yes: that's how we dress when we're ruined," said she*

the rhythm of her voice canting along, as if narrating a book to a child, acting out in disparate voices

> *"Some polish is gained with one's ruin," said she*

the country girl and the ruined one, back and forth, I cannot tell which she relishes being most: the one who doesn't know what it means to be ruined but is fascinated

> *"True. One's pretty lively when ruined," said she*

or the one who drags out ruin through innuendo and lark, the word like a match struck and flaring with new meaning each time it is sung out

> *"My dear—a raw country girl, such as you be, Cannot quite expect that. You ain't ruined," said she.*

Wanting to hear L's voice, I call her number at a payphone, wait the rings, listen, until on the other end I hear her husband bleat: *Stay away from my wife!*

Want to remember L saying she loved my hands, had watched them play guitar in the school hallway, had wanted to hold them, saying they were good hands, but can only remember early mornings curled around my guitar, strumming in an empty hallway, heart racing whenever footsteps sounded around the corner.

L gifts me a copy of Nick Hornby's *High Fidelity*, says the scene where they have sex in the car during the father's wake was more real in the book than in the movie.

In the book they don't go through with it because neither one has a condom.

About another English teacher at our school, L says she only took me out to lunch (burgers; talk of *The Celestine Prophecy*; ideas of synchronicity) because *she's lonely, lonely a long time, probably wants you, I'm surprised you didn't pick up on any of it.*

Wanting to share a poem I have just written about shaving while listening to a Bukowski poem being read on the radio on his birthday, I mass email a group of friends.

    L messages back right away saying this particular date is significant for other reasons: Buk's birthday, Elvis dying, and *our own kind of anniversary.*

Want to know what is going on as I sit in a coffee shop in Corpus (having said nothing to L about being in town for winter break, proud of this, but also worried about this) only to have her storm into the place and ask for a phone book at the counter.

Later, I will try to recall what she wore and get lost thinking she was dressed like a teacher and not knowing what that means. Right now, I am stuck wanting to look up and also not wanting to move. This feels like a test, like I have done something wrong in establishing boundaries. She also looks mad, out of breath as if in mid-argument.

Before I can do anything, she looks around, spots me, then quickly accepts the book being handed her, and steps back outside.

[two]

Want to talk about writing a book focused on ideas of the devil, and when I say so, my professor interrupts and asks: *The devil or the double?* Which makes us both laugh, and someone between us says: *Who is the devil but our double?*

L gifts me a copy of James Joyce's *Ulysses*, tasks me to read the last fifty pages, that *we are there*, only I find there is no punctuation, no cease to the voice.

    I end up reading only the dirty parts, which feels incriminating at first, then eventually misguided, as I cannot see myself anymore.

"if I can only get in with a handsome young poet at my age Ill throw them the 1st thing in the morning till I see if the wishcard comes out or Ill try pairing the lady herself and see if he comes out Ill read and study all I can find or learn a bit off by heart if I knew who he likes so he wont think me stupid if he thinks all women are the same and I can teach him the other part Ill make him feel all over him till he half faints under me then hell write about me lover and mistress publicly too..."
    — *Ulysses,* episode 18

Want to believe she wouldn't be so bold as to have me finding these words that feel as if they incriminate the both of us, that *we are there* bluntly and messily and crudely said.

Then I remember that the book is written by a man, that a man created Molly and Molly's voice is some part of Joyce, some fantasy/wish fulfillment mixed with reality probably, but all within what a man claims to understand of a woman, which can never be anything but an approximation, a guess and gesture informed by societal narratives of gender roles.

Joyce created Molly, shaped a person to be what he needed them to be, in words that I look over wondering what is being asked of me.

Want to share that I see it now as a kind of grooming, what Joyce did in creating Molly, what he says through her, what her character says about what men think women are like and what men think women want.

Also, what Joyce says through her about *how* men think women want, that they are all body, all "acquiescence, self-abandon, relaxation, the end of all resistance," while the men in the story are all mind, directive, control.

What Molly wants from her young poet, how she settles for her husband, what the patriarchy has done to all involved, generations of readers included, the way the book is canon, a classic—all a grooming into place of human experience as heteronormative.

I notice that each *if* in Molly's speech is speculation driven by want and realize I have my own list of *ifs:*
    If it hadn't been for my hormones.
    If I had only walked away.
    If I had only transferred classes.
    If I had had any self-restraint and awareness.
    If L had had any.
    Maybe then it wouldn't have happened, maybe then it wouldn't feel like it was all my fault.

Wanting to go to work during a blizzard because the coworker I crush on (despite living with someone else) might be there (I learn the term "work-husband" much later and think, *That's what I was!*), I put on my coat in my apartment in Jersey City, tuck a book, a pad of paper, and a pen close to my body, then trudge down the middle of snow-covered Summit Avenue, and only make it two blocks before a gust of wind lifts me up in the air, holds me there for a whole three seconds—after which I land as if pushed back, and decide to go home, call in to work where my coworker says: *Jesus, J, only a Mexican would try to go work in this weather!*

    I learn later only a person who has had boundaries blurred would fall to blurring them himself.

    Later I see only a person unable to work out the source of their unhappiness would try to go work in any weather looking for an excuse.

    When I hung in the cold air, for a second, my heart belonged not even to myself.

Wanting I-don't-know-what, I continue to type an ex's password and check her email for months after we stop dating. One day I read an email where she shares with a friend about her and a new guy and I want to forget everything.

    How did I become a creep? Worse than that: How did I find it so easy, so natural, to abuse the trust I was given? And to what? Hold on? Hurt myself?

    Later, I never repeat this kind of controlling and intrusive behavior.

    I find other ways to hurt myself.

Wanting to "do it right," I spend seven hundred dollars I do not have the first time I go to a strip club. The last dancer in the VIP lounge sits on my lap, asks me what I do for a living. My friends from college coach me to say we are young professionals, ask me to dress the part, button-ups and slacks, to say I am a broker, a financial advisor, I even look up what an actuary does, how they are *experts in uncertainty and use mathematics, statistics, and financial theory to measure, manage, and mitigate financial risk*—I memorize all this, but still say poet. We sit silent. I read the names tattooed on her thigh, names on a ribbon, names across a heart.

    I feel like I am failing my friends.

    I feel like I am failing L.

    I feel I was not made to be worldly, only wordy.

Wanting again to be worldly, I ask the street artist in New Orleans back to my hotel room. I am in town to give a speech at a conference about how a scholarship that covered only one year's textbooks in undergrad changed my life. Instead, I read a poem about being broke in South Texas after undergrad, then skip out on the rest of the conference to walk around the French Quarter.

    I meet her by stopping to look at her art. She has a laugh that *shakes the rain down*, I write later. As we both take off our clothes, she stops me to say she can only go so far: *I've got something.*

    I say nothing needs to happen.

    Later, she runs a bath, lights a cigarette, and tells me how this would be easier if I were a woman.

    If I were a woman, would I be like L?

    Would I have the swagger and conviction she had walking into the hotel room in Texas?

    It feels like failure to be a man in a hotel room only able to wonder how any of this—the bodies, the vulnerability—could be easy.

Years later, the street artist reaches out to me on Facebook, shares a photo of her holding up a printed copy of a poem I shared with her. Her message is brief: *Is this yours?*

I decide to ignore the message—I'm in a relationship, plus there are several ways she could find out if the poem is mine with just my name, the copy she's holding has my signature even—but not without feeling that I am being shitty and failing again.

A poem can ask one to do some work in understanding its nuances by being vague and using ambiguous language. A poem can do this because it is inherent in its nature; consent is a given. When people try to act like poems, it is a decision, one often made without consent.

I think of her message again: *Is this yours?* I know the answer is yes and no. Yes, I wrote those words, and no—the image of the worn piece of paper, the memories brought on by the faint impression of her hand—I cannot say I consent to them.

My tía and I are heading over to Jay and Chris's. They have an apartment in a nicer part of town and going there means I'll get to hang with Jay and be called "tough guy," which I like.

In my eyes, Jay and Chris are so glamorous, they could have their own 80's style sitcom. Chris, the charming Delta Burke-style lead, and Jay, the laid-back dude quick with the jokes. My tía and I could be their neighbors. Jay and I could hang out and he could teach me to live up to "tough guy" status.

Jay always has sunglasses on, aviators with a dark tint giving way to a clear view of his cheekbones. That and his short-sleeve button ups and hair in a pompadour-style cut—I think it's everything that is cool. Cool, too, how he talks to me like a WWF wrestler psyching out the competition by hyping himself up.

Perhaps I think sitcom because of how much my tía laughs with them. The only other time she laughs like this is when I put on my mother's gym clothes and march around the house. I am never afraid of her hurting me or making fun of me when we are at Jay and Chris's. She is another person completely, which means I can be too.

Later, I can't remember when we stopped going over nor why. I also can't remember the moment when it clicked that Jay and Chris were both biologically women. I only know my tía laughed a little less on the weekends. I only know Jay was the kind of man I wanted to be.

I meet Jojo over at Jay and Chris's.

Jojo is Jay's nephew and is spending the summer with them. He's about my age, which is why I am invited to sleepover one weekend.

Of hanging out, I only remember feeling tense, already afraid of other boys, of being bullied, made fun of. Jojo is taller and skinnier than me, which I both fear and envy. We probably watch HBO, which is a big deal because we don't have it at home.

What I remember is the tension of sitting at the table during meals. Jay and Chris looking sternly at Jojo asking him to eat.

Jojo staring down at his plate, not moving. The food there changing meal to meal, like words he can't get himself to speak.

Jojo retching in the bathroom at night.

On the last morning, Jojo eats a few small bites of potato and eggs.

Jay tips down his sunglasses—the only time I can remember him doing so, his eyes smaller than I expect—and saying *thank you* so softly to Jojo I almost miss it.

Minutes later Jojo walking to the bathroom. When the door closes behind him, Jay raises his voice to yell *Goddamn it!* and leaves the table to smoke outside.

The silence between Chris and me is broken now and then by Jojo's retching and harsh breathing.

Want always to be seen as the Greek statue one girlfriend compares me to in college (when I would run five miles each morning, then eat an apple for breakfast, and nothing else til dinner).

Want the friend who gasps then grabs my T-shirt, who in her fist pulls the fabric tight around my torso so that enough of it is in her hand the shirt feels like light on my skin, who then loosens it, letting the fabric hang off me as it would on a clothesline, who whispers: *Jesus, J, where did you go*—want her to always be asking this, for someone to always be asking this, so I feel the apple turn in the empty space I am and feel proud.

Want the friend who says I need to *Cut it out* as we are in the gym lifting weights after a run, who tells me how others are beginning to talk, want him to say it, what he means, to quote what others are saying about me, but he only says *Cut it out*, and *Don't act like you don't know you have a problem*, because I know that he will never say it, that I will be left alone to hurt myself because we are both men and men don't do what I am doing so there is nothing to talk about, nothing beyond a gnashed core where there was apple and now only remains hurt flesh rotting to the color of my skin.

Starving myself, all I care about is: Would L like my body now? Would I be wanted now?

A woman tells me she read to her sister from a journal I left at her house the night before, says: *I wanted her to see who you were to me.*

Later it makes sense to think I had left the journal wanting to see who I am to women. Their attention, L's attention; their approval, hers.

Projections and blurred boundaries—my self-worth, my self-esteem, my very words at risk of being lost.

Wanting I-don't-know-what, I take two different women to see *Eternal Sunshine of the Spotless Mind*, the movie where a man and woman pay to have each other erased from each other's memories.

I wonder what L would think of this movie, then ask each woman at the end of the night what line they think is my favorite.

One says: "I don't know. I liked it when she said too many guys think she's a concept and she completes them, and says she's just a fucked up girl."

Later, I realize I am not looking to hear myself figured out, I am looking for who they think I am.

Because I don't trust myself to know.

[three]

[three]

Want not to look back, like I look back on the woman who comes to my room one night in college and stays, settles into my arms watching a movie, says she knows she can trust me not to try anything then quickly falls asleep, and long after, so do I—

like I look back on the woman I want to keep laughing, so I agree to go to my first college house party because she is going, my roommate and I dressed nice: button-ups, ties, cologne, I ride with her in her Jeep, and she lets me keep making her laugh, only when we get to the party she gives me a quick look back (I think perhaps shame, or maybe my tie) and leaves me at the door—

I spend the night walking up to people I recognize from classes, but not knowing what to say—

at one point, I sit on the stairs, and two women sit behind me, one says: *I swear, I need to have someone inside me by the end of the night—*

later, the woman I came here with stumbles drunk into my arms, I find myself carrying her to her Jeep, stopping in the middle of the street when I notice snow beginning to fall, I tell her so (*look, it's snowing!*), and she mumbles something I can't hear—

when we get to her car, she stands up, says she's fine, frowns, and drives us home in silence—

like I look back on the woman who keeps kissing and undressing for me, has my mouth where she wants every afternoon, who stops me and sternly says she will not have sex with me, which is fine, I say, because I have not asked her to, yet I am here, bared and doubted—

the one who speaks of having engaged in evangelical dating in the past and has me wondering if that's how she sees me: secular, in need without knowing it, malleable—

the one who I drive to the mountains one morning, walk with her out into a clearing, and in the cold morning light grasp and kiss desperately, and even there at what feels like the edge of the world, I can see my breath rising, heavy, almost laughing, almost saying out loud: *See all the sex I'm not having with you!*—

like I look back and want to never have said to one woman: *Don't sleep with him, I want to be your first!—*

she repeats this back to me the next day when I can't remember calling her up or anything about the conversation beyond this statement, these words, I know I meant them but can't believe I said them aloud—

the words repeat when I think of her now, her voice reciting my words back, as if they are a headline she cannot believe—

like I look back on the woman I kiss while drunk, immediately regretting it, she pushes me off and I apologize and others begin talking, so I run through the streets, run until I am at the window of an ex, and I go in—

like I look back on the ex who later says that she had her way with me that night, only I can't remember her putting on the condom for me, only remember my fingers tapping on the windowpane and her name on my lips like an apology—

like I look back on the coworker I kiss and whisper dirty things to that keep her giggling and holding onto me in a bar while my then-girlfriend waits at home, this, another night before leaving a city and holding onto another's body as if to leave an imprint, a trace, wanting to be remembered, wanting to remember—

like I look back on the one poet who I listen to talk about her boyfriend, who is intoxicating to talk to so we keep the conversation going: from workshop to café—

to abandoned bridge where I deny wanting to kiss her after she says she likes me, that I am dangerous, and I say let's keep talking, we're over a river, rivers are connected to everything—

from barstools to poems written side by side, to her bedroom and the startled sleep we share—

to the awful shit I half-remember saying drunk one night, asking in the darkness for her to go down on me, getting shitty and upset when she says no, me saying she wouldn't understand what it feels like after so long, then falling asleep pouting—

Did I really say that? I'm so sorry—

to when she finally does, nights later, do it, and it is awkward, she seems not timid, and not afraid, but so far away from me, I feel like shit for years—

to when another poet who knew us both at the time confesses to me later that she told him she only messed around with me for so long out of pity, she felt she had to, *you wanted it so much,* I feel the river we talked over sway the bridge again—

like I look back on every conversation I have with women that leads me to pleasing them in ways that are awkward to say point blank (*knee over jeans, with mouth over fabric, with fingers right before introducing me to their parents*), pleasing them and them just leaving after, not wanting complicated, not wanting to be anything—

like I look back on the men whose bodies I have touched and who have touched my body yet who never kiss me—

one a middle school friend and we are watching porn and he suggests it would be good to touch ourselves then each other, that it would feel good and wouldn't be gay of us, and I say yes but only if we both take turns, only I do it more because he asks me to, wants me to so bad, and I want him after so many years of being hurt by him, his insults to me in front of others, his questioning of my sexuality through jokes, to accept me—

only there isn't time for that because my mother opens the door to my room on a night he's sleeping over and finds us naked—

there isn't time to get dressed, I don't remember getting dressed, only remember apologizing to her, trying to explain over her sobs and cries of how ugly and wrong it is that it doesn't mean anything, her getting louder—

the tone of her voice the same as when I had to go to the hospital for a deep cut in my arm a year earlier, a dismay and dirge for me and not-me, as if she worried not that I would die but had died already—

there isn't time for me to die or get dressed or to explain anything, she is lost, crying over the person I was before she opened the door—

the other man, a college friend who is queer, who shares with me his dismay and disgust at straight people's homophobia, intentional or not—this is before I have the words *micro* and *macroaggressions*, the words *sexual fluidity* and *spectrum*, only know the words of empathy, of seeing and consoling a friend lost in feeling insulted, marginalized, othered, and who himself didn't have the words for the want in his eyes, the want to be accepted as is—

    who one night in his dorm room while lying on his bed begins to inch his hand closer to mine (like I have inched my hand with women) and when I don't move begins to inch further onto my body so that when he touches my penis I feel a need to protect him, begin to hear him in my head, his voice saying *accept me, don't reject me, don't hurt me*—

    and I know he is not actually saying this, I can only hear his deep breathing, yet I know what I do in this moment could break him and our friendship apart, so I touch back wanting him to accept me, only he guides my hand to his penis and I feel cold—

    I feel I am in the van again with L, the ocean crashing in the distance, I know I have to answer to his vulnerability but also am shocked into my own—

    later, after I pull away, he goes back to judging my taste in women, in music, in writers, etc. as he always has and continues being wounded by straights and saying that he has no one who

understands him while I follow him into stores and
readings and restaurants and cafés hoping he still
likes me, trusts me —

like I look back on the man who does try to kiss me, a high school friend who I at one point had reason to call out for bullying and manipulating me and others (bullying in that he would pick apart my taste in women, music, and friends, only to later hit on the same women, claim the same music, befriend the same friends; manipulating in that there came a point where there was not one woman in our friend group who hadn't slept with him or had to physically push him away) and whose response was to mock me: *How am I bullying you? How am I bullying you? You're just so sensitive!—*

we meet up years later at a warehouse party and end up alone in another warehouse sitting around a camping lantern and he shares how he had what he insists on calling his "first gay experience" recently, says the phrase like it's a brand, that he is still sleeping with a lot of women, of course—

I say *that's great* and we sit in silence a little too long, I begin to feel he wants to kiss me, but it isn't until another night that he tries—

after a party he takes me to, a party where I do not know anyone and yet am left alone by him as he seeks out the woman he wanted to meet up with, and so I begin talking with people, find a woman who wants to go into nursing and I tell her I teach at Del Mar and can help her get started with their nursing programs, only her fiancé, who I learn after is a marine, just returned from tour, stands behind me ready to slam a beer bottle into my head—

after we drive away from the party, my head bleeding, my friend taking the marine's side somehow, and me offended that he does so, offended that this would even happen to me, *I'm the next hot new writer, who the fuck is this guy?!?* I yell to him, to no one, to the universe lit by the passing streetlamps—

after I get out of his car, he gets out, goes to embrace me, and I, thinking it's a hug, lean in and turn my face only to feel his tongue scrape against my stubble—

in the orange streetlamp light I realize I am another on his list, another experience he is chasing after, forcing, I am having to push him away—

wanting not to look back like this because I cannot make it all cohere, not to toxic masculinity and what it would have me be like, not to L and her expectations of what I should have gone into the world and been like—

cannot reconcile anyone's intentions nor predatory inclinations to the varied whims and impulses of want, that want is something shared between us however differently cast—

cannot move forward without acknowledging the shame that attaches itself to each experience of want—shame that has me silent, changing stories to mask as straight, omitting details, afraid to fully trust my queerness because other queer people have hurt me and because straight people hurt queer people—

    afraid to trust women because I don't know if they actually trust me or feel compelled to go along because I am a man, and it's not trust or love but a power dynamic being enacted—

    afraid to have women afraid to trust me, knowing that they have reasons to fear men—

    afraid to trust men, their judgments, their wants, their indifference, their impatience, their capacity to harm—

    afraid of myself, of what this self might actually be made of—

cannot move forward without feeling myself in part defined by being unable to forget while also being unable to clearly remember—

cannot move forward without acknowledging the fear that I have things wrong, that I misremember, and if not misremember then misunderstand, the fear that it's my fault, if only I had done things different, acted different, been someone completely different—

    fear that has me lock and relock every front door I have ever slept behind, that obsessive want, that lifetime want to never have something go wrong, that I must always be responsible, it's on me to keep it together—

cannot move forward without feeling myself
defined in part by the weight of needing to know
who I am blurred with the weight of not knowing
what I have been to others—

what am I then: what is my knee, what my mouth, what my hands, what my fascination and wonder, what my boyhood trust that made it easy to want to get close to people, what my adult tendency to want to create distance from others while also being wounded by the isolation, what my absence and silence to those who would get close, what my vanity to appear mysterious and aloof while only being at best polite, if terse, and at worst chronically wounded—

what am I to the exes, to the almosts, to the drunk kisses, to the friends embarrassed for me, to the friends who gossip about me, to the ones who deny ever touching me, to the ones I don't talk to anymore, to the ones I wish I could apologize to and the ones I wish would apologize—

what am I to the teacher who had her virgin poet
and sent him off, asking him to keep his silence—

what am I then, but this complicated silence—
     this need to name what happened tangled in the fear that to do so would mean that it happened—
     this push to face the wound suffused by the fact of the wound—

[four]

Want to remember more from Sunday school than peeking at the teacher's bra when she leaned over to pass wafer pieces to practice for my first communion—which makes me a cliché, of course, unoriginal in my sin.

    Want to remember more, but only hear L's voice: *See now how it tastes.*

My babysitter, sixteen, strips me down first, then herself, then asks me to place my mouth on different parts of her body. I know from movies my uncle has shown me some of what is expected of me. My babysitter only stares and waits as I tug at my five-year-old manhood, hardening, stubbornly muttering: *No, no, I can make this work.*

I think of this moment later: L pages me one New Year's Eve and I wait on a street corner, glass of champagne in hand. She picks me up shortly after midnight from a party and we drive to the beach, where I wake up in the backseat with L working her mouth on me. When I realize I am not going to be able to finish, I run out into the sand, throw my hands up in the air, and scream.

Want to be Sonny Corleone in the scene from *The Godfather* where he beats up his sister's husband who has been beating her. I watch in awe as Sonny drags the bastard across the street, pummels him, kicks and crashes a trash can over his head—that I could do the same to my mother's exes.

    Like the one who was younger than my mom and would hit her. Or the one who dragged her down the backsteps of the house and wouldn't stop until the neighbors called the cops. Or the one who I heard whispered about when we first moved to Texas, the one who came at her with a knife. Or the one who was a tow truck driver and hooked us up with tickets to a monster truck show, and who later cheated on her despite him being the ugliest one.

    This is the one who whispers *let him listen, let him learn* one night as I tiptoe in the hallway unsure if what I heard was sex or violence.

Wanting what I don't have, I wait until I am alone at a party, the other kids off watching TV in another room, then slip two large stacks of comic book hero cards into my pockets, then wait outside on the porch to be found and taken home.

After a while, I hear raised voices behind me: *Where are they then, mom? If you didn't see him take them... I know he did, they're poor!*

Later, when my tía catches me organizing the cards in my toy crate under the kitchen sink, she yanks me by the arm and walks me to the stove, the flames already rising, waiting for my hand.

Wanting to prove a point to my tía who hits me with whatever is in her hand, I place a dead cockroach on the forehead of her newborn son.

    I remember not finding it funny, nor that it felt at all like revenge; there was a darkness to the insect's body that felt like the tail end of a feeling.

Want to remember singing to my grandmother her son's favorite song—remember how I used to walk around proud to say I know five for sure things about my father, one of them being his favorite song was "Querida" by Juan Gabriel—how I learn it on my guitar quickly when I hear she is in the hospital, how my mother considers it *afrentoso* to bring my guitar, and I say no, there's a reason—how I work out the Spanish on my rough tongue, how I sing to my grandmother, how she rocks in her hospital bed saying: *Que lindo, que lindo*—how I don't know or care what others in the hospital think of me playing, only that I want to play, keep her rocking, part of my face reflected in her clouded eyes that cannot see me, eyes that tremble at the chords and words—I swear, sometimes all I can feel is music.

One uncle shows up once a year in the middle of the night, banging at the door. Sometimes he asks for money, sometimes he asks for news about his son who was taken from him to live with another man.

     Never in my childhood do I hear the mother speak about the father, yet I can hear it in the voice of his son, my cousin, who, when he asks a question now, is barely noticed, his voice low, barely there, and who, even when people ask him to, never repeats himself.

Another uncle asks me not to tell anyone, then sits me down with a Sprite, strips to his underwear, and puts on a porno. I sit on the floor; he lies on the couch.

  This scene repeats another time later.

  I am used to family in their underwear; it's South Texas, it's hot. What I don't know is what I watch pass between men and women, what comes out of their bodies, what sounds, what fluids. I think it beer for a moment.

  I was four, and later, when I admit this to someone, they ask: *Why beer?*

Wanting to fly in the air like my favorite wrestlers, I climb the dresser and launch myself towards the bed, only to miss, and spring back with black eyes.

Later, calls from Child Protective Services.

I have gone to school before with welts and bruises from being castigado yet not one phone call. Belt lashes across my back are kept hidden under a T-shirt.

These bruises are new, my fault, but visible.

The attention has me in the air again.

Want to visit my grandmother's grave in Mexico as I had been told we were going to; want to visit because she is buried close to my father and I have to this day never seen my father's grave; want to but am dropped off instead at my tía's house, my father's sister, because my mother's boyfriend wants to go to the beach and I can't find the words to speak up.

    I bury my head into my tía's bed and pretend to sleep, though it is only four in the afternoon; though I am hungry, thirsty, I am too angry to care.

    The next day, my tía wakes me, hands me photos I have never seen before of my father. She asks if I could write a poem for her. I write lines about working hard, about the moon and the stars, all in English, then translate the whole thing into Spanish before handing it to her.

    The memory now is how quiet the world felt as I moved words around and hearing myself say: *Perdóname por todo lo que no puedo decir.*

Wanting a comic book at the 7-Eleven, I turn to my mother and ask for it, only to have her say no. Later in the car she explains why: there is no money, and it will be like this for a while.

    I sit in the orange light of the parking lot, calm, no longer kid-sad over the comic book, on some level realizing I am being asked for something I need to learn quickly how to give.

Later, when the woman who was the babysitter dies and I am near forty, my mother shares that she was actually my cousin. She was the daughter of a tía I didn't know I had, a tía who suffered from mental illness. My mother isn't more specific, just a sense of pity and shame hanging between us on the phone.

My mother shares she went to the daughter's wake, says there were a lot of strange people there, that the woman had grown and come out as queer, married another woman. I have just recently begun understanding my own queerness and feel myself want to hide at the word *curioso*, at the way my mother speaks of what I now know is a queer crowd of mourners in a tone of judgment that always comes up in conversations related to queerness.

Before I can think of anything to say, my mother asks me to not be angry with the woman, to forgive her, that anger can poison a heart.

She asks me for forgiveness as well, for not knowing about the abuse, for being young and not knowing any better, for not having any other choice in what to do with me.

Want to understand what it means to be in my room as a teenager listening to my cousin Sylvia talk with my mother and my tías in the living room.

Sylvia is a year older than me and I am always compared to her, in grades and in personality. She is brighter in all ways, for sure, and I admire her when I am not wincing from my mom and tía's praise of her, praise I envy, praise in which I am implied as not deserving.

It is summer and Sylvia is pregnant and debating whether to go back to high school or not. Instead of the rejection and judgments I thought she would receive, the women of the family embrace her, welcome her with a solidarity that I also admire and envy.

Want to understand this feeling of listening as my cousin Sylvia is accepted by my family in a way I know now I will never be. I will grow older and move away and feel more and more distant from my family.

Meanwhile, this moment for Sylvia is a rite of passage, something my family can understand from their own experience of having pregnancy interrupt, surprise, shock, and alter their lives.

This they understand—not the books nor black clothes I kept around me, not the education nor the modos and coraje they said I walked around with, not the white girlfriends I brought home, not the distance nor the college degrees—

Want to understand so that I can reassure myself that it isn't bitterness I feel, not anger or jealousy, just a depression, a disappointment, a despair at the thought that life means nothing if I am not accepted—

Part of me says: *Here is proof you will never be accepted—*

What else could it be? Why else would my mother keep asking when I will give her grandchildren? I will hear this question in college. I will hear this question years into my first marriage to a white woman who squeals over the idea of having children. I will hear this question years into my second marriage, years into my partner being diagnosed as chronically ill and disabled and unable to have children. I will explain it to my mother over and over again across the years that we can't have children, that her question after grandchildren is a wound she keeps opening—

Want to understand why I cried to myself as women embraced and consoled my cousin in a way I knew was important and celebratory and also meant I will always be here on the outside.

Want to remember my own voice as my mother recalls it when she tells the story of staying with distant family who begrudgingly host us as we made our way to Corpus Christi from Matamoros, family who let us stay in a toolshed, who cooked meat one night, and left the kitchen window open, so that the smell reached us, and one of the first words my mother remembers me speaking is the Spanish for meat: *ca'nita, ca'nita, ca'nita—*

    She repeats the words fast for comic effect, so that I only hear them in her voice, cannot catch any strain of the voice I had once, so insistent, so full of want.

My tía, perhaps wanting to make me laugh as she did when I was younger, perhaps just wanting to break the silence, makes references to "el chile" and "tronando huesos."

It occurs to me years later that she is my sense of humor. That I know how to laugh through tears because of her, make puns and fake bravado because of her. Her toughness and crude jokes stand in for machismo, teach me about the world through innuendo, guide me toward what is expected of me as well as how to survive it.

She asks me about college, warns me: "Si no lo usas, se te va caer"—*If you don't use it, it'll rot off.*

We are driving between Matamoros and Corpus Christi in the early morning, also like we had when I was younger.

Only this is after L.

This, along with my tía asking if I am staying out of trouble, has had me silent for miles.

[five]

Devil or Nothing:
An Abandoned Manuscript

Who is the devil but our double? As a question, this is demeaning. As if you should already know the answer it's so obvious.

That said, trying to come up with an answer is, shall we say (and we shall) *tempting*:

Time to devildown.
I devil-dog dare you.
Devil or nothing.
Make mine a devil.

In the Rider-Waite tarot, you see me as looming over a man and woman who stand tall as my knees, naked with chains around their necks. You see me as sitting with my right hand raised, palm facing out. You see me as posed in an almost Vulcan salute, can almost hear Spock's greeting: *Live long and prosper.* To you, I appear confused, caught as if in greeting, as if in recognition of the man, the woman, and you, the viewer, stuck as if not knowing what else to do—this moment is what you turn to for answers?

Transparency: you get caught staring at how the word *spare* is held there in the middle, simultaneously said and visible while also unsaid and invisible. Like what it feels like to say *the devil made me do it.*

Language is how you get lost. You give over your attention to presence that cannot be held—while elsewhere, at the edge of a garden perhaps, the flowers and trees are marked off, and the dirt begins to feel less special.

Did you hear the one where I split an apple with my hands a week before my wedding night and let it rot under the bed?

When the night came, apparently, I waited for my fiancé to fall asleep, then held the halves under her nose all night, so that my history, what I am capable of, would enter her.

In order to dig to hell, you must believe.

The heart is deceitful above all things, says the Bible.

    Perhaps it only feels like deceit. Perhaps it is only clouded, confused.

    The heart only does what it was made to do: whatever it needs to go on.

Except for your sins, you'd have nothing to talk about.

Eternity would be one long summer afternoon, mad green flies gathered at the window screen, singing their wordless blues against the mesh between you and the outside world.

Each dust mote, each bit of scurf, each eyelash dark as a flake of ash tumbling from your life has its own kind of flight—a fall, really: an insistent and wingless descent.

You wish it were easy, good and evil, gods and devils. The deceitful heart who created the world different from the one set to destroy it.

You wish it were easy, but remember you are created in the image of one, tempted in the image of another.

You look like the creator. You are your own destroyer. You wish and you wish.

Change names. Change tongues. Change countries.

Under one sky, you pass your days.

You cannot change enough.

Memory is composed of mites, bedbugs, lice, exes, mosquitoes, words spoken you wish them back, words unspoken you wish them on the air, and other creatures which graze upon the human body indiscriminately. What remains is less than dust and marrowless, yet you fester and heal, fester and heal, and so on, until neglect or indifference keep the soul in place.

In the Tarot of the Spirit, I hold my arms up in V's like to scare children, a downcast sword in the left hand, in the right hand a hole in the palm. The rest of me remains undefined behind a black circle with a pillar centered, chains out around the torsos of a man and woman. The man looks away off the card. The woman looks at the man. I remain here at the center, content, in anguish, waiting to see what card you pull next.

The old devil in your tía throwing whatever she had in her hand at you.

The old devil was never to be trusted. All that deception and fire. The tail and finely groomed beard. The red flesh. Dante's frozen three-headed monster. All too much.

In ink, you feel, like him, born from the brightest of lights, to be turned into darkness.

Like him, made to change your ways so others can be justified.

Be darkness.

But look how you rise, how honest, how sincere, in the eyes of others. The word made flesh, the flesh put to paper.

Each drop of ink gleams with some of the darkness you walk in.

Moonlit earth. Toads and roots. All you are, pulsing.

The old devil in your mother talked into punishing you with a belt by your tía, saying you need, for once, to know they both think you are in the wrong.

This, when you are a child.

The old devil in the weight of the belt as your mother closes the bathroom door and begins to lash across you, she could be the ocean, angry, come to fight you.

The old devil in your face as your mother pleads for you to understand, to stop making her have to hurt you.

Things are carried out in the old devil's name as well, a name often also taken in vain.

Like Him, the deceitful heart keeps its silence, keeps you guessing, defining yourself in the wind.

You go on, and know nothing of a love so great, him and Him seethe waiting to see who answers first.

You as a child pulling out the liner notes of a Brujeria tape and seeing, instead of the words to a song, a photo of cocaine bricks, and propped there as if just rolled into place, a man's head, severed, the old devil in his eyes, in his mouth, a dark line moving when the cassette pops to a chuckle.

From canvas to canvas, the tail of the old devil keeps moving. Long, impossible smile. An arrow for an end, the target keeps moving: now up, now down. Each painting, a clock with only one hand: even I can't divine the impossible hour.

The old devil in your father the one night he struck your mother and she grabbed you, walked you out the door, out of his life for good. The old devil catching up to her in the hands of boyfriends who considered themselves artists and every other night would go on a high and paint your mother's face with fists. The old devil who keeps saying *every man knows the same art.*

The old devil in the metallic taste on your tongue as you jolt and jar against the wall to steady your drunken step down the street, repeating your name until you find yourself looking around, lost on a street that is suddenly nameless.

Think: Stars, those lights held high above you, are dead inside.

In the Archeon deck, I am a card of half-darkness, half-light. At the center, alone, I stand sideways, arms crossed, as if about to turn away, my torso and face pulsing red on the card in front of you. I sport a goatee that fits some of your expectation; the soft shadows that line the rest of me do not. The suggestion of skeletal wings, and of legs either horse or goat—you can't focus for too long before you come back to what you were expecting and how it isn't here. No chains, no man or woman, only horns, a sideways glance. Only the impression of an argument being had nearby. The impression that I am caught forever acknowledging the argument because no one else is around to do so.

You keep talking of hell as somewhere else. Look around: the lying tongue, the hard stare of moths, skin—all the devils are here. Even words carry on the wind, move across the bones in your ear. At the core, you are fire.

Consider me just another lost yet hopeful soul. Consider the years, the attention I give to the living with each page. Consider these words prayered into the rest. Consider prayer as the last word in incompetence.

Flies linger, want perhaps to see scars, not able themselves to heal like we do: a closing, a change of hue, a ruin of seashell color. You see them everywhere come summer, even on the black screen of your eyelids, in the pulse of blood: there is no real way to be free.

Transparency: you get caught staring at how the word *spare* is held there in the middle—

A spare word of advice: Don't talk to your woman about other women. Do so, and you might as well throw a baby into the deep end of a pool. Sure, in time they'll float and keep alive, but that is all they'll do.

Transparency: you get caught
in the middle—
might
as well
float and keep alive

When whatever it is settles in you. When death becomes a reversal of the gaze. When the eyes you used to keep sight over things are now below you, a site for this other sight, I will still be here, my transparent wings robing the flies.

[six]

Both uncles mentioned above have reputations for stealing.

They also have moustaches.

My father died in a prison in Matamoros. I share this fact freely with people, sometimes regarding my creative work, sometimes just so that they know more about me, but it isn't until I am in my thirties that it occurs to me that in hearing this information some might consider my father a criminal. His being in prison for me has always just been part of a story.

Like my uncles: when I say I grew up without any positive role models, I mean them and my mother's exes (of which my father is one, too). They are deadbeats. That my mother left my father after he raised his hand to her makes him a deadbeat, too.

I have often talked of growing a moustache only to have women shut the idea down. Which I get, sort of. I've heard it's creepy, cringe. There's even the meme that says growing a moustache is *the sluttiest thing a man can do*, which is the kindest take I've heard.

When I do grow one, my partner, who has had her own protest about it before, lets it ride. She has been supportive in so much, someone who has learned with me over time. We have learned to give space to each other, if only because we're curious enough about the other that we want to see what happens next.

I find myself sharing with close friends that I am going for it mainly because on a practical level I don't appreciate the feel of chin hair on face masks. I end up sharing that it brings up a lot, that I've been wanting to rock a 'stache for some time, been afraid to, not just because of the associations, but also because I end up looking like my father, who I didn't know, who died young but not without asking for forgiveness from my mother.

He might have asked to be forgiven for hitting her, or for threatening to steal me away from her, or for naming another son after himself so that I have a half-brother out there who is also *José Angel* like he was, or for dealing drugs which is how he ended up where he was.

I don't know what he asked forgiveness for because he asked for it when we visited him in prison and my mother pulled him away to talk. I was left to the side only able to catch *perdóname* repeated in a difficult rhythm amid the chatter of other men having their own difficult conversations in that difficult place.

My partner tells me I have not shared any of this with her before, that she feels like an asshole now. I tell her I did not know the words for it all until now.

Through this lived experience, the moustache gains another association: inheritance—but of what? Of creepiness? Cringe? Violence? Depravity? Inarticulation? Sluttiness?

Or is the moustache shaped like a bird, always in flight over what a man says, what he can't take back, what he can't control?

Have I inherited a capacity for witness as well as want?

My father's last words to me keep getting lost in the din of every argument between a man and a woman.

[seven]

Wanting to talk more with L, I bring up getting sundaes which is one of my ways of coping with stress in high school (among other things too boring and obvious to get into). I share this with L after a school function where I played classical guitar for a fashion show, plucked etudes and waltzes as young bodies modeled clothes.

This is the first time riding in L's minivan, talking all the way to the T-heads, talking as we look over Corpus Christi Bay. I tell L about how hard it is to live at home, all the arguing between me and my mother, my mother and her boyfriend, all the while my tía spelling out how I should hurry and move away for college. Because if I don't I will go crazy.

I don't know when L starts holding my hand. I find it rough, the way she keeps kneading into my skin with her thumb as I repeat what my tía said: "Si yo estuviera en tu lugar, ya me habría puesto una pistola en la cabeza."

L asks what it means, so I translate, roughly: *If I were you, I would've placed a gun to my head long ago.*

Wanting to keep her smiling, I spend a class field trip to San Antonio taking photos of L. I wonder what it looks like: white teacher and brown student taking turns posing for photos.

I realize now we didn't take turns: it was L in her shades at a table smiling; L talking to someone, her eye catching me in her periphery; L in her shades in a hotel lobby. I thought she was brilliant to wear sunglasses all the time, that others couldn't tell what she was feeling.

What I was feeling: a strong dread of going back to where I live, back to being seventeen and so inarticulate I had to write a note to my mother asking her not to bring another man into the house to live with us, worried he would beat her like others had. Back to being the stunted boy I was after having read her the note and have her response simply be: "Yo mando; voy hacer lo que quiero." Or as I break it down for L: *I'm in charge, I'll do what I want.*

What I feel now: that I have always been wanting to hold still, to slow down, to recover. That as a marginalized person, I can't. I am always in survival mode, like my mother has been. No time for photographs, those documents that exist outside the before and after of a moment.

What I feel now: that this moment between my mother and me taught me how words can mean nothing to someone and yet still defy that nothing by their presence.

One photo still comes fully to mind: L with a leg up on a bench, arm on her knee, beaming at me like a hunter posed over a kill. This image remains locked in my mind, perhaps because the before and after of that moment had her doing what she wanted and asking of me what she wanted, but for that moment, that moment caught by me and later destroyed at my whim, the world held us awkwardly, fervently still.

One day our history teacher breaks down how our high school was built as an answer to desegregation: namely, to keep the Mexicans out of the white side of town.

None of us know what to do with this information.

This teacher, who for a month has been suffering from an irritation in her eye and wears an eye patch, goes on to say this is why a city official recently said publicly that our school is unfit for anything other than training auto mechanics and nurses, that we have produced no artists or writers of any value.

I think of this teacher, a white person only able to see half the room, only half of the brown faces, who maybe didn't see my restless face looking around quickly before writing down in my notes: *Try to see what she sees.*

L jokes about how she hated me when I first entered her classroom, thought me another ego-driven snot who would put no effort into English.

Wanted then to never meet L's daughters, worried that I'd end up in a Greek tragedy.

Now, I just want to know how close to my age they are.

Want to remember how this ee cummings poem came into my life but can only imagine L reading it aloud:

may i feel said he
(i'll squeal said she
just once said he)
it's fun said she

      Not sure why she shared it; all I can hear now is how the gender roles were reversed for us.

(may i touch said [s]he
how much said [he]
a lot said [s]he)
why not said [he]

      Enough repetition, and the roles blur. Reading on, I feel my eyes water, feel my skin itch

(let's go said [we]
not too far said [we]
what's too far said [we]
where you are said [we])

      And like that I am a teen in the classroom again, painfully aware of how other students shift in their seats when I pass—

may i stay said he
(which way said she
like this said he
if you kiss said she

      I never knew what they knew about what went on between us nor how much, if at all—

may i move said he
is it love said [he])
if you're willing said he
(but you're killing said [he]

      nor why exactly I can envision her leaning with one hand on my desk

but it's life said [we]
but your wife said [we]
now said [we])
ow said [we]

      her face away from mine, I cannot see what the class might have seen

(tiptop said [we]
don't stop said [we]
oh no said he)
go slow said she

      only feel the hum of her voice down my arm again, her hand an inch from mine.

(cccome?said he
ummm said she)
you're divine!said he
(you are Mine said she)

My mother surprises me one summer afternoon when she looks over from the driver's seat and says: "Cuidado con esa señora."

Meaning L.

High-school-me pretended not to hear.

I flip it all over in my head now—*Be careful with that woman*—and note that the English has nothing of the age implied in the Spanish, lacks a certain uncanny knowledge.

L comes to an open mic with her husband, and both watch me read a poem about a blue dress she wore once for me.

The blue dress was worn to a city-wide honors ceremony. The poem started with her telling me this and me not knowing what to say.

A local newscaster was there as a guest host, ended up making a joke about my last name sounding like it had "goose" in it, that people called me "the goose."

The poem becomes one of the ones I memorize by writing it out by hand over and over, the heat of the words summoned with each recitation.

I later share about the newscaster making this joke when people ask me how to pronounce my last name—no, *really* pronounce it. Meaning they want to hear me say it in Spanish. Meaning they are white and not satisfied when I say it's ok to pronounce it English, ah-ruh-gooz. Meaning they are likely to say "oh, like goose?"

The poem becomes one that I pride myself in performing randomly in public. Like when I first meet people and they learn I am serious when I share I am a poet and look at me as if I had just introduced a lamppost as my father. Like to crowds of people waiting for a show to begin. Like at an IHOP at 3 a.m. when our table has been ignored for longer than I feel is right.

When I tell people of the newscaster's joke—and believe me when I say I have had more than enough opportunities to share about the joke—sometimes I say that I kicked him in the shin as I crossed the stage that night. Some part of me knows it's a lie, and another part wonders what I can trust of that night.

    The poem becomes one that I begin to worry is a curse and not a spell. One that becomes more embarrassing to associate myself with the more I recite it. One that I can't think of even now without cringing at every syllable my body remembers feverishly summoning and chasing after.

Want to never be the old boyfriend L rants about as she speeds down Ocean Drive: a writer, close to her age, he missed his mother's funeral because he was working on a novel.

She tells me all this while jabbing her finger in the air: *That better be a great fucking chapter!*

Want to make sure each word in a letter I write by hand is clear, I bear down, often retracing words, at times piercing the paper.

Later, L exhales as she says: *I love how you darken certain words, go over them again and again.*

L gifts me an anthology of poems with the words, *For the man who loves my 'pilgrim soul'* inscribed on the first page.

Later, I find the Yeats poem these words come from, hold my breath when I read the lines "But one man loved the pilgrim soul in you, / And loved the sorrows of your changing face."

After, I write the poem out by hand, memorize it.

L smiles one afternoon as I get into the passenger seat, laughs as she tells me that as she walked out the door her husband had said, straight-out: *Don't sleep with J!*

L turns down a street lined with palm trees, takes her right hand off the wheel, waves it in the air as she says: *I just couldn't believe God had sent you to me in the first place, and a virgin—I couldn't pass it up!*

Wanting to strike all the right notes as I sit in front of my guitar teacher's desk, I play a newly memorized piece for him, only to have him bark out: *Steady your hands! You play like a virgin!*

Wanting I-don't-know-what, I spend most of prom writing into my notebook what I think could be poems. In middle school, I rewrote the lyrics to songs on the radio with my own words, but never thought those poems.

Tonight, I write about *auburn hair* and *sunlight*, about *beauty* and *love* and *darkness*, about *stars* and *trees*, using phrases like: *the trees are skeleton calliopes.*

Later, I read to L from these pages and she holds her breath.

Later, I read from these pages for my psychology teacher and she says: *Gee, kid, you've got some issues.*

Wanting no one to see my gut, I spend my childhood and teens under oversized T shirts.

Even at the beach, I wear the wet, heavy fabric like a flag of shame. Cousins laugh, my tías say: *Mira,* and I look down and see the fabric shaped to the folds of my teenage body. *Llantas,* my mother calls them, tires made of brown skin, brown flab doubled on itself.

Wanting no one to see my want, I hide chocolate bars in my room. I open the drawer and find them, the Snickers' brown wrappers bright as the wet skin I keep hidden, each bar as wide as a fold I blame myself, my mouth, my body for, a fold I am sure is family—my mother who wraps a black trash bag around her torso, then begins pedaling on the exercise bike in the living room, the plastic breaking with light and dark as she turns to me and says: "Tenemos que enflacar"—*We must thin ourselves down.*

Wanting to look big and play the part, I ask L to drop me off in front of the hotel so I can run in and pay for the room with money I should have been saving for the plane ticket to college.

Then, I didn't notice how driving to the hotel together meant driving past the projects where my family first lived, the side of Corpus we could afford then, the side of Corpus known around the city in jokes and warnings about sex workers, drugs, poverty.

L tells me to crank the A/C, *that's all I care about.*

L pushes my hands away and begins to undo the buttons of her dress herself, pats my chest, asks me to *slow down, enjoy this as I do.*

L whispers that I am seventeen, yes, but soon I'll be eighteen, and eighteen will go on and have romances, and eighteen will go on and wear condoms (not like this first time, don't worry), and eighteen will tell her all about the world I go and see—but eighteen will not talk about this, yes?

Wanting to remember the feeling of me and L's bodies together as I wait afterwards outside the hotel for a friend to pick me up, I begin to think the sun a symbol for unbuttoning a shirt, of hair being let down, of wanting to talk about a secret—and at the same time wanting to keep it a lousy, fucking secret.

Want to remember every word spoken, every gesture, but I can only keep coming back to L whispering: *Keep this to yourself,* then gripping my hand so hard there is no room to speak up.

Epilogue

Epilogue

I keep coming back to what L said after I first spoke to her about another woman. I was doing so because she had asked me to, said eighteen should leave her and see the world, have romances. Quixote with a Moleskine and a whiskey sour. Quixote turned Chicano creep. What L said after: *Don't talk to a woman about other women.*

Yet some women asked to hear specifically about L. Not sure what I said exactly. Might've said patronage. Affair. Married woman. High school English teacher. Senior high school English teacher. Teacher. Might've said going back to Texas was tough. A woman twice my age. I was lost.

I have tried for years to write about this, and always hear L's voice: *Eighteen doesn't talk about this.* All I can do sometimes is talk about it to myself. Go over it and over it, at turns doubting myself and hating myself. Doubting how I handled it and am still handling it; hating myself because I look back sometimes and see it as all my fault: *If it hadn't been for my hormones. If I had only walked away. If I had only transferred classes. If I had had any self-restraint and awareness. If L had had any.*

I wish I had asked why she sent a photo of herself when she was my age in college dressed like a black cat for Halloween (this, with the copy of *Ulysses*). Was she as unhappy in her life as I was in mine? Long before I ever breathed, at least, she was happy. I wish I knew the people who hurt the people who hurt me.

Self-restraint and awareness worked itself out for a while on social media. Messages I did not respond to. Blocking L. Unfriending. Eventually, there was another email from L congratulating me on a poetry prize. I didn't know what to say. I still don't. Once we had sex, there was no going back to her being the benevolent teacher. Which is what made the Broadway show gesture such a crucible; I didn't know who I was supposed to be: student, lover, boyfriend. I didn't know who she was smiling at me like that. My body only knew it had to return the smile.

What does it mean to have written this book? Is it all over? L and I are not a story because stories have endings. Unfriending and blocking on social media is not an ending. An unanswered email is not an ending. Silence isn't exactly a closed door.

A friend asks me if I ever consider moving back to Corpus Christi, if I miss my family.

I cannot move my thumbs fast enough to respond to his text so I end up sending a voice recording of me rambling about how my partner and I do think of it now and then, that we could live there, sure, but I say that I don't think Corpus can live with us, our queerness, our needs. That I left because there was so much going on with my family, so much that they needed from me.

As I spin out words, I keep in mind that this friend is like me: he is Mexican, a PhD, surviving in a big city which means navigating white spaces while feeling isolated and without community. I feel like I must sound fierce, must make clear our narratives of distance and survival have been worth it.

I surprise myself by saying that my family no longer needs me to go back, at least not go back and live there. My brothers are grown up, my mother is safe. They didn't need me for any of it.

He says later that it was soothing to hear my voice and words, that I am the only other person he knows who has left and stayed away as we are.

I wish I had said *of course I miss my family, every day. But who are they now and who do I remember? Who am I and who do they remember? I could move back and still not be there.*

I do not understand what L means to me, but I do understand Jojo. I understand him being afraid, afraid of his body and afraid of doing anything and yet needing to do something to have control.

I understand another friend who grew up in Corpus Christi, who I saw at a Renaissance festival, of all things, down by Ocean Drive, dressed in all black except for the purple velvet on one side of his cape, and dancing to Madonna's *Ray of Light*. I was dressed like a priest, a Halloween costume I thought hilarious and appropriate for the event, and thinking everything of my friend's dancing in the summer Corpus heat and humidity, being himself, being a dance.

I understand another friend who I met years later, a friend who invited me to read at the university he works at in New York, who had gone to school in Corpus Christi and had heard of me and my work from a man who lived there and ran a café I used to go to. This friend remembers Corpus fondly, the food and the ocean, but at times seems wary of the memories. He shares that he had been harassed for being a gay man and I remember thinking I couldn't forgive my city for that.

I understand Jesse, the older brother of the babysitter, who, when I was a child, lived in the back of their house. My mom and tía would whisper to stay away from him, that he was not safe to be around. Which made me look at him a little longer when I would see him around: take in his curly hair let out to grow and curl in a way I still can't let my own hair do, and his eyes, the lashes long and dark, and, on some mornings, what I know now was eyeliner at the edges. He kept his distance as if he knew what my family had said about him, what his family had said, he seemed a man haunted, nervous in his own home.

I say I understand and mean compassion and friendship in a way that isn't a puzzle, something to work at like a mystery.

Even for the man who tried to kiss me, who after we had fallen out, and right before I was about to leave Corpus again for New York, I ran into at a bookstore one last time. He shared with me that a mutual friend of ours, someone we had gotten drunk with and laughed with and jammed with, had died, had overdosed, told me this through wires keeping his jaws sewn shut, his lower jaw having been shattered by a fight at a party the week before. I understand him and pleaded with him, told him that I was leaving and that he should leave too, that this city was going to kill us, surprising myself by saying this and feeling it to be true.

No mystery to work out, just fear and acceptance, ruined selves and wanted hopes.

Then there's Yeats, his "old and grey" poem, and the mystery L had me solve. I look back and it is a bit of vanity, no? To quote it in a book, to have me search for it. And yet, who doesn't want to be remembered fondly? The years I spent reciting this poem to myself, I marveled at the imagery: how everything seems to blur together and dissipate to stars.

Notes

Pg. 17: This passage includes a quote from the short story "Araby" by James Joyce.

Pg. 19-20: This passage features an interpolation of the Thomas Hardy's "The Ruined Maid."

Pg. 29-30: These pages include references and interpolations from James Joyce's *Ulysses*, specifically episode 18.

Pg. 142-4: This passage includes an interpolation of the poem "may i feel said he" by e.e. cummings.

Pg. 150 & 173: These pages include references to the poem "When you are old and grey" by W.B. Yeats.

About the Author

José Angel Araguz, Ph.D., is the author most recently of the lyric memoir *Ruin & Want* (Sundress Publications) as well as the poetry collections *Rotura* (Black Lawrence Press) and *La esperanza espera* (Valparaiso Ediciones). His poetry and prose have appeared in *Prairie Schooner, Poetry International, The Acentos Review,* and *Oxidant / Engine,* among other places. He is an Assistant Professor at Suffolk University, where he serves as Editor-in-Chief of *Salamander* and is also a faculty member of the Solstice Low-Residency MFA Program. He blogs and reviews books at *The Friday Influence.*

Other Sundress Titles

Little Houses
Athena Nassar
$16.00

In Stories We Thunder
V. Ruiz
$12.99

Slack Tongue City
Mackenzie Berry
$12.99

Sweetbitter
Stacey Balkun
$12.99

Cosmobiological: Stories
Jilly Dreadful
$16.99

The Valley
Esteban Rodriguez
$12.99

the Colored page
Matthew E. Henry
$12.99

Year of the Unicorn Kidz
jason b. crawford
$12.99

Something Dark to Shine In
Inès Pujos
$12.99

Slaughter the One Bird
Kimberly Ann Priest
$12.99

What Nothing
Anna Meister
$12.99

Where My Umbilical is Buried
Amanda Galvan Huynh
$12.99

www.ingramcontent.com/pod-product-compliance
Lightning Source LLC
Chambersburg PA
CBHW071116160426
43196CB00013B/2593